DATE DUE

$16.00

Wheeler, Jill
Corazon Aquino

MEMORIAL SCHOOL LIBRARY

001308012
Wheeler, Jill   B Aqu
Corazon Aquino

LEADING LADY

CORAZON AQUINO

**Written by:
Jill Wheeler**

Published by Abdo & Daughters, 6535 Cecilia Circle, Edina, Minnesota 55439.

Library bound edition distributed by Rockbottom Books, Pentagon Tower, P.O. Box 36036, Minneapolis, Minnesota 55435.

Copyright©1991 by Abdo Consulting Group, Inc., Pentagon Tower, P.O. Box 36036, Minneapolis, Minnesota 55435. International copyrights reserved in all countries. No part of this book may be reproduced in any form without written permission from the publisher. Printed in the United States.

Library of Congress Number: 91-073025   ISBN: 1-56239-082-1

Cover Photo by: UPI Bettmann
Interior Photos by: UPI Bettmann
Page 31 Photo by: Pictorial Parade

Edited by: Rosemary Wallner

TABLE OF CONTENTS

Mrs. President 5

Learning to Work and Pray 6

School in the U.S.A. 9

A Politician's Wife 11

A Prisoner's Wife 14

Fighting Back 17

Tragedy in Manila 18

Cory for President 23

Taking Charge 27

Visiting the U.S. 29

A Rough Road to Travel 29

February 25, 1986 Maria Corazon Aquino was sworn in as the seventh president of the Philippines.

MRS. PRESIDENT

On February 25, 1986, Maria Corazon Cojuangco Aquino was sworn in as the seventh president of the Philippines. At age 53, she became the first woman ever to hold that office.

Wearing her trademark yellow dress, Corazon, or "Cory," as she is known, placed her hand on the Bible and took the oath of office. "I would like to appeal to everybody to work for national reconciliation, which is what Ninoy came home for," she said.

Ninoy was her late husband, Benigno Aquino, Jr., who had been murdered three years earlier. Cory Aquino had followed in his footsteps to lead her nation to freedom. Under her, Filipinos, residents of the Philippine Islands, enjoyed democracy for the first time in 20 years.

LEARNING TO WORK AND PRAY

Aquino never thought she would become president of her country. She was born January 25, 1933, in Tarlac Province on the island of Luzon, 50 miles north of the Philippine capital city of Manila. She was the sixth of eight children.

Like many Filipinos, Aquino is of mixed descent. Her father, Jose Cojuangco, was of Chinese ancestry. Her mother, Demetria Sumulong, was of Malaysian ancestry. There also was Spanish ancestry in Aquino's family. Her name, Corazon, is the Spanish word for heart.

The young Aquino was fortunate because her family was wealthy. They were among the few Filipino families who owned large tracts of land. Because of their wealth, Aquino's family was active in politics. Her father and her brother served in the Philippine congress. Her mother's father and an uncle were senators.

At home, Aquino's mother was loving but strict. She told her children they must work and pray. When Aquino was six years old, she entered

Saint Scholastica's College, a private Catholic grade school in Manila. She did well in school and was popular among the other students even though she was very shy.

As she grew, Aquino learned many things about her native country. She learned that the Filipino people have been struggling for freedom for centuries. The Philippines, a chain of 7,100 islands, were conquered by Spain in the 1500s. The Spanish conquerors took most of the land and forced the Filipino people to work it for them for very little money. In 1898, Spain signed the islands over to the United States.

In 1942 when Aquino was just nine years old, the Philippines were conquered again, this time by Japan. It was World War II. The U.S. fought to get the Philippines back, and Manila was bombed many times in the struggle. Aquino's home was burned in the attacks, so she and her family went to live with their grandparents. Finally the Japanese surrendered and the U.S. regained control of the Philippines in 1945.

A year later, on July 4, 1946, the U.S. gave the Philippines its independence. But the newly independent country had many problems. Most Filipinos were poor. Because of all the bombings, the country was in a shambles and over a million people had been killed. Rebel groups tried to overthrow the new Philippine government. Because of these problems, Aquino's family moved to Philadelphia, Pennsylvania, when she was 13 years old.

Japanese fighter pilots bombed the Philippines during World War II.

SCHOOL IN THE U.S.A.

In the U.S., Aquino enrolled at Ravenhill Academy in Philadelphia. A year later, her parents returned to the Philippines, but Aquino and one of her sisters remained in the U.S. to finish their educations.

Aquino went to high school at Notre Dame Convent School in New York City, where she lived with an aunt. She graduated at the top of her class and was noted for her quiet strength and deep faith in God. In her senior yearbook she wrote, "It is up to you to bring to the life you are entering, to the state you must help to form, an energy of true religious faith."

Following high school, Aquino earned a degree in French and mathematics from the College of Mount St. Vincent in New York City. In between classes, she traveled to the Philippines to spend her summers and holidays with her family.

During one of those holidays she became reacquainted with a young man named Benigno "Ninoy" Aquino. She had met him before when she was nine years old, but she had not been interested in him then. "What does a nine-year-old girl feel about a nine-year-old boy?" she said later about their first meeting. "I remember Ninoy kept bragging he was a year ahead of me in school, so I didn't even bother to talk to him."

When they met again, Ninoy was a handsome young journalist and law student. The two exchanged many letters during Cory's senior year at college. She was impressed with his letters because they were "not mush, for one thing."

The fall after she graduated from college, Aquino enrolled at Far Eastern University's Law School. She planned to earn her law degree, but Ninoy had other plans for her. The two were married on October 11, 1959.

A few months after the wedding, Ninoy bought some land in the town of Concepcion in the Philippines, where he had been born. While he cleared the land to begin farming it, Cory lived in Manila with her mother-in-law. By that time she was expecting their first child.

When the farm was ready, Cory arrived, bringing their new daughter. Ninoy already had gotten to know many of the people who lived near their farm. The people were encouraging him to run for mayor of Concepcion.

A POLITICIAN'S WIFE

Ninoy listened to them, and at age 22 became the youngest mayor in Philippine history. He had begun his career in politics and Aquino saw very little of him then. She accepted this as the way their life had to be. She had been raised to believe that women stayed home and raised the children while their husbands were out working.

Ninoy continued to follow his political ambitions. He became governor of Tarlac Province, where he managed a plantation owned by Aquino's family. During his time as governor, Ferdinand Marcos became president of the Philippines. Ninoy did not like the new president. He and many other people believed Marcos was corrupt and that he was destroying the freedom of their country.

In 1965, Ninoy ran for a seat in the Philippine senate. That election saw much corruption. Wealthy candidates sent friends out into the country to offer peasants money in exchange for their votes. This way they could be sure they would be elected.

Aquino helped Ninoy campaign for the senate. Now a mother of four, she traveled around the country speaking to crowds. "I am the wife of Ninoy Aquino," she would say. "I'm sorry he can't be here, so I have come in his behalf." While Aquino and Ninoy campaigned, Marcos continued to criticize Ninoy. But Ninoy won the election and took his seat in the senate.

As the nation moved into the 1970s, the situation in the country grew worse. Marcos was accused more frequently of using the government's money for himself and his wife, Imelda, and of using the military to silence any opposition. Students, workers, peasants, clergy, and women's groups took to the streets in protest. They protested the Philippine system of land ownership where 10 percent of the people controlled nearly 90 percent of the country's wealth. They said the Marcos government had too much power.

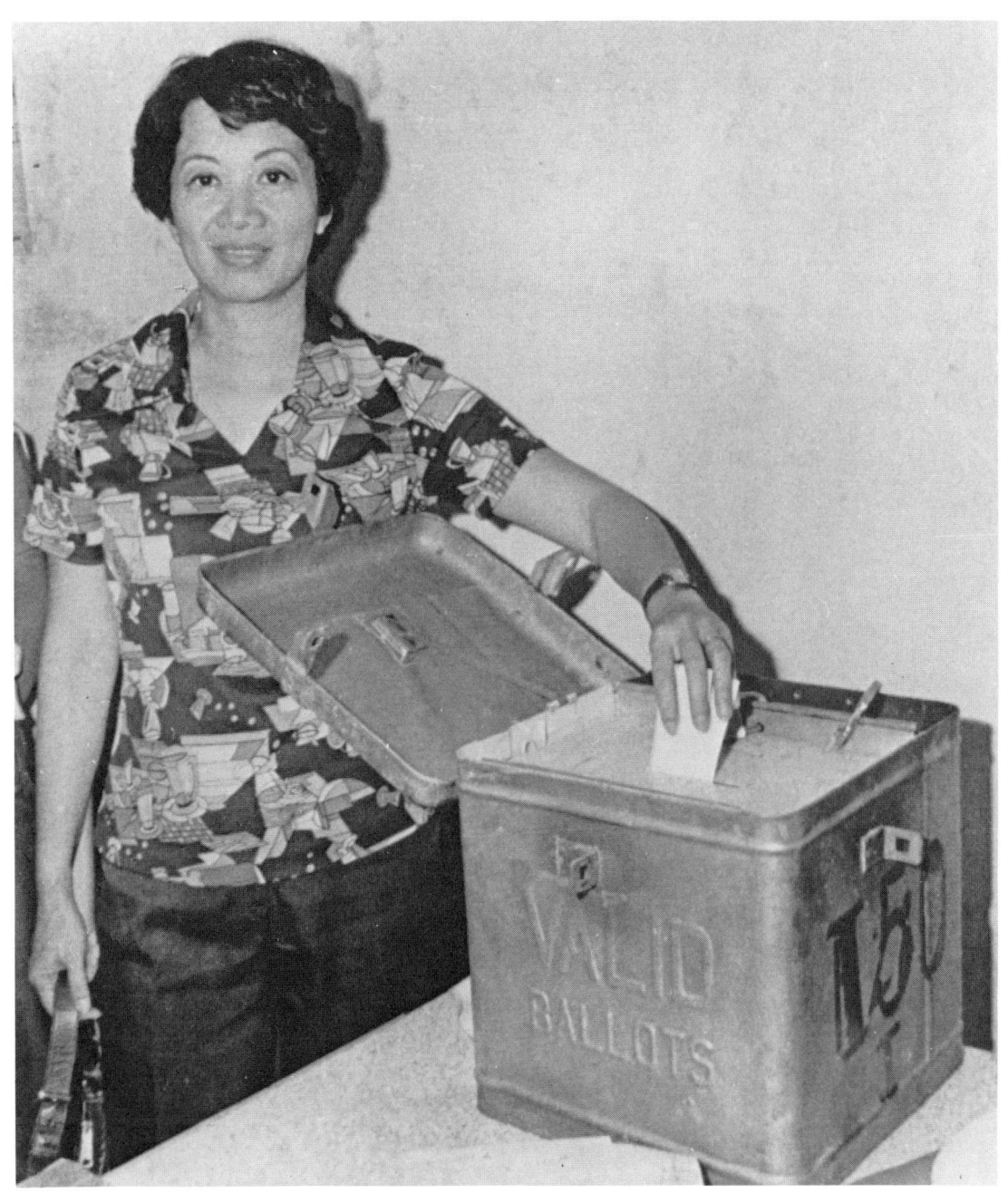

Aquino helped her husband, Ninoy, run for the Philippine senate.

President Marcos used the protests as an excuse for instituting martial law in September 1972. Martial law is temporary rule by the military. In martial law, citizens have no say in how they are treated. Many people believed Marcos ordered martial law because he suspected Ninoy was going to run for president in 1973 and Marcos feared his opponent would win the election.

The day before martial law was imposed, police arrested Ninoy at a hotel where he was meeting with some other members of congress. Ninoy was just one of many people arrested and sent to military compounds in the next few days. At the same time, the Marcos government closed newspaper and magazine offices, and shut down radio and television stations. They placed all media under military control.

A PRISONER'S WIFE

At first Aquino did not know if Ninoy was dead or alive. She took her baby daughter with her and visited every prison camp she could find and asked if Ninoy was there. The guards at the camps laughed at her and made her sit outside in the hot sun or pouring rain. It took her more than a month to find Ninoy.

Ninoy remained a political prisoner for the next seven-and-a-half years. During that time, Aquino visited him every week, often bringing their five children with her. She learned to stand up to the authorities and request better conditions for Ninoy. She even spent some nights in his cell with him, sleeping on the bare dirt floor.

Aquino said those years were years of growth for her. "Perhaps that was the greatest education of my life," she said. "In the past, I had always lived such a sheltered life, such a comfortable life."

As she grew more confident, Aquino also became more active in politics. She was the eyes, ears, and voice of Ninoy while he was in prison. She kept him informed of what was happening in the government and carried messages between him and the other leaders of his political party.

Aquino helped fight her husband's battle against the Marcos regime.

FIGHTING BACK

While Ninoy was in prison, he was convicted by a military court of murder. He refused to participate in the trial because he said the charges were false. He went on a hunger strike to call attention to his plight. For forty days, he drank only water and the vitamin-filled liquids his wife brought to him. At the same time, Aquino took their story to the global news media.

Two years later, the military court found Ninoy guilty and sentenced him to be executed by a firing squad. People around the world were so angry with the verdict that Marcos was forced to halt the execution. Yet Ninoy remained in jail and became weaker and sicker.

In March 1980, Ninoy suffered a heart attack. Aquino petitioned to have him released from prison so he could have heart surgery. The permission was granted, and the family flew to Dallas, Texas, where Ninoy was operated on successfully. Following his surgery, the family moved to Boston and lived together for the first time in nearly eight years.

Aquino said the years in Boston were some of the happiest of her life. She was again a wife and mother. Ninoy lectured at several universities and kept a close eye on the activities in his native land.

TRAGEDY IN MANILA

In 1983, Ninoy could stand it no longer. He decided to return to the Philippines to run for a seat in the congress. He knew the death sentence against him remained, and knew he probably would be arrested as soon as he entered the country. He also had heard Marcos' health was failing, and he thought it was time to make a move.

Aquino was one of many close friends and advisers who tried to talk Ninoy out of returning to the Philippines. But Ninoy would not change his mind. His plane arrived in Manila on August 21, 1983, and was met by a crowd of supporters. As soon as he stepped out of the plane, he was killed by a gunshot to the head.

Aquino and her family returned to their homeland for Ninoy's funeral. Two million people marched in the funeral procession, and Aquino asked people to help her find her husband's killers. "If only one or two or three of you can show courage at this time, others will follow, and the truth about Ninoy will come out," she said.

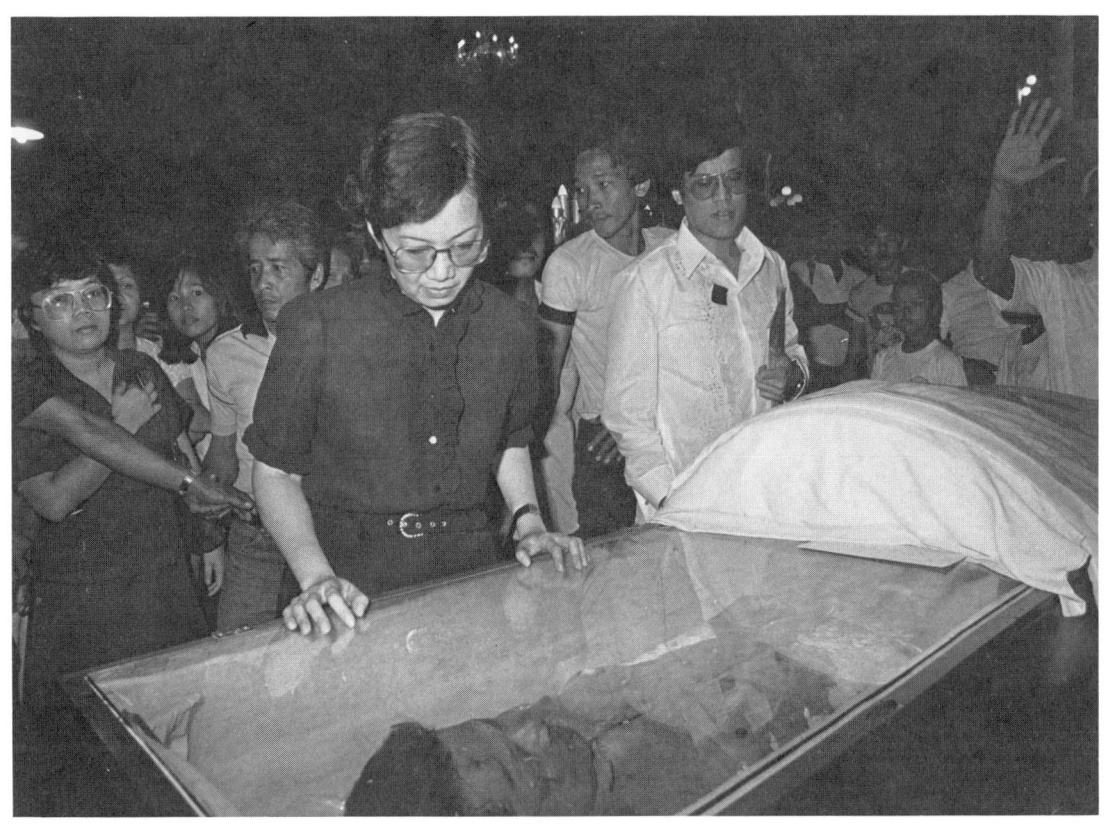

Aquino offers her final condolences to her husband who was tragically assassinated by the Marcos regime.

Many people encouraged Aquino to continue her husband's fight for democracy. Her friends said she seemed to have changed since Ninoy's death. She had become confident, stronger, and willing to speak out at rallies and call for Marcos' resignation.

As the 1984 elections approached, Aquino was actively speaking across the nation urging the people to vote. Thanks in part to her work, her party, called Laban, won one-third of the seats in the congress. Laban means party of the people.

After the elections, many people told Aquino she should run for president. They thought she could beat Marcos. In October 1985, she was speaking before a University of the Philippines sorority when audience members asked her to run for president. Before she knew it, she said she would if two conditions were met. The first was that President Marcos call a snap, or quick, election. The second was that a million people sign a petition asking her to run.

Aquino crisscrossed the Philippines asking people to vote against the Marcos regime.

Aquino vowed to work for freedom.

CORY FOR PRESIDENT

No one thought Marcos would call for a snap election because it was not in the country's constitution. But that November, under pressure from the U.S. and within the Philippines, he called for elections in February 1986. A month later, Aquino was presented with a petition for her to run for president with one million signatures. True to her promise, she filed the papers for her candidacy and listed her occupation as "housewife."

Aquino began campaigning immediately. She did not believe then that she could beat Marcos, but she knew she had to try. She convinced a man who had planned on running against her to be her running mate. Together they crisscrossed the nation campaigning

Aquino began wearing yellow dresses, the color of the Laban party. She vowed to work for freedom, saying, "When I saw (my husband) in his coffin, with bloodstained shirt, I promised him I would continue the struggle for justice." Often she campaigned 16 hours a day, flying from island to island.

As the election drew near, everyone was excited. Huge crowds gathered to hear Aquino speak. They shouted her name over and over. The color yellow was everywhere. Aquino began to believe she could win after all.

The eyes of the world were on the Philippines on February 6, 1986 – election day. Aquino went to her home of Tarlac Province to cast her vote. "Today is my day," she told reporters. "I hope to see you at my inaugural." She was just one of 24 million Filipinos who voted that day.

Many people were concerned Marcos would cheat on the election to make sure he was named the winner. On that day, there were reports of ballot box stealing, buying votes, scaring people away from the polls and violence. Most of these violations were reported on Marcos' side of the election. Some government employees helping count votes were so upset with the election fraud that they left their jobs.

Two days after the election, all of the votes still had not been counted. Marcos said he was the winner. Aquino disagreed. "The people and I have won and we know it," she said. Finally, the vote counters said Marcos had won.

Aquino would not accept defeat. She organized a rally in Manila and called on people to protest Marcos' victory and refuse to buy things from businesses that Marcos owned. Several weeks later, two powerful members of the Philippine military led a revolt against Marcos. The men, Defense Minister Juan Ponce Enrile and Deputy Armed Forces Chief Lieutenant General Fidel Ramos, said they revolted because they wanted the rightfully elected president to take office. That was Aquino.

The Catholic Church also threw its support behind Aquino, Enrile, and Ramos. Church officials urged the people of the Philippines to do the same. Marcos ordered soldiers to go after Enrile and Ramos, but thousands of Filipinos took to the streets to stop the tanks as they rolled toward the rebel camps. The soldiers would not fire on their own people, and the tanks turned away.

Three days later, Marcos held an inauguration ceremony. Aquino did the same. That night, Marcos, his family and some supporters left for exile in Hawaii. He had been forced out by Aquino, his people, Enrile, Ramos, and the U.S. government.

Aquino put together a strong cabinet of advisers to run her party.

TAKING CHARGE

Aquino's work had only begun. Many of her people were poor. They wanted land, food, and jobs. Rebel groups still threatened the peace. She asked the people to be patient, saying, "You people were so tolerant and patient under Marcos for 20 years, and here I am only two days and you are expecting miracles."

Aquino immediately began to put together her Cabinet of advisers and ministers to help her govern. She included people from several political parties and encouraged them to put aside their differences and work for the good of the country. She refused to live in Malacañang Palace because that was where the Marcos family had lived. She even appointed a man to recover the $2 billion in Philippine money the Marcoses had stolen. "It is time to heal wounds and forget the past," she said.

Aquino found being president very difficult. There was much work to be done, and because she was a woman, many people did not take her seriously. She said she did not want to be called "Mother of the Nation." "I will remain a mother to my children, but I intend to be Chief Executive of this nation," she said. "And for the male chauvinists in the audience, I intend as well to be the Commander in Chief of the armed forces of the Philippines."

Aquino was upset early in her presidency that her election had not been officially recognized. People said her presidency was illegal because she had abolished the charter under which she had been elected. She had abolished the charter to cleanse the government of Marcos' influence.

To legalize her presidency and restore democracy to the people, Aquino pressed the Filipino lawmakers for a new constitution. She said the constitution was "for our children so that they can live in freedom, so that we shall never have another dictator." The constitution established a two-chamber legislative body, much like in the U.S. It also limited the president's power to declare martial law, and arrest and hold political prisoners. Finally, it provided for a six-year presidential term for Aquino.

VISITING THE U.S.

In September 1986, Aquino made her first trip to the U.S. as the Philippine president. She visited four cities in nine days, beginning with San Francisco. Nearly 1,000 people gathered at the San Francisco airport to welcome her with cheers of "Cory! Cory! Cory!"

Her next stop was Washington, D.C., to meet with President Reagan and address a joint session of Congress. Many of the members of Congress wore yellow ties and tossed yellow roses in her honor. Her address to Congress began and ended with standing ovations. Later, Senator Robert Dole of Kansas told her her speech had "hit a home run." She replied, "I hope the bases were loaded."

A ROUGH ROAD TO TRAVEL

While Aquino has made many strides in returning democracy to the Philippines, many people say she has not done enough. Some members of the military disagreed so much with her policies that they staged coup attempts. A coup (pronounced Kōō) is when the military tries to take over the government. Since her election, there have been more than six coup attempts.

The worst of the coup attempts began on December 1, 1989. Two thousand rebel soldiers tried to take control of the country by taking over the headquarters of the Philippine army, a Philippine air base and a television station. They fought against soldiers loyal to the Aquino government with guns and bombs. Finally, at Aquino's request, the U.S. sent several fighter jets to help stop the fighting. By the time the uprising ended, 46 people had died and another 200 had been hurt.

Aquino survived the coup attempts, but she did not punish the people responsible. Her critics say that is a mistake, yet she has always believed in peaceful change over violence. Only time will tell whether or not her peaceful policies will allow her administration to survive.

She also faces the problem of educating her people about democracy. "Filipino people came from a dictatorship and went to a democracy," she said. "What people would like is to get the best of both worlds." Her government still struggles with the fact that for poor Filipinos, food and shelter are more important than democracy.

In addition, most members of the Philippine congress are landowners who do not want to share their land with the peasants who have been working it. This has made it virtually impossible to pass major land reform laws. Aquino's own family plantation, Hacienda Luisita, has come under fire for the way farm workers are treated. Several members of her family also have been accused of using government money for their own benefit.

U.S. President Reagan and Philippine President Aquino.

Aquino's presidential term expires in 1992. She has said she will not seek re-election. However, her soft-spoken, peace-loving nature has forever changed the face of her country. Aquino proved that democracy can triumph over dictatorship. She showed how people can unite to improve their country.

President Aquino as mother and grandmother.